I have been interested in Bullsh*t from a very tender age. (I grew up on a farm.) I always did extremely well at school. (I passed.) I sought to understand the meaning of life. (I went to university.) I have worked as a university tutor, a barman, a storeman, a clown, a drama teacher, a researcher, and attempted to make money out of building and selling houses. (Translation: I am an Australian writer.) My first novel, *Undercurrents*, is a gripping psychological whodunnit thriller—a sometimes funny, sometimes poignant, gut-wrenching page-turner. (Translation: please buy that book too.)

THE
COMPLETE GUIDE
TO
TRANSLATING
AUSTRALIAN
BULLSH*T

REN LEXANDER

Angus&Robertson
An imprint of HarperCollins*Publishers*

For Geoff, Jeff, Geoff, Rob, Mike and Lindsay
for no good reason (translation: for lots of fun bad reasons)

AN ANGUS & ROBERTSON BOOK
An imprint of HarperCollinsPublishers

First published in Australia in 1990
Reprinted in 1992
CollinsAngus&Robertson Publishers Pty Limited (ACN 009 913 517)
A division of HarperCollinsPublishers (Australia) Pty Limited
25–31 Ryde Road, Pymble NSW 2073, Australia

HarperCollinsPublishers (New Zealand) Limited
31 View Road, Glenfield, Auckland 10, New Zealand

HarperCollinsPublishers Limited
77– 85 Fulham Palace Road, London W6 8JB, United Kingdom

Copyright © Ren Lexander 1990

National Library of Australia
Cataloguing-in-Publication data:

Lexander, Ren.
   The complete guide to translating Australian bullsh*t .
   ISBN 0 207 16695 1.
   1. English language—Australia—Terms and phrases—
   Humor. 2. Australian wit and humor. I. Title.
427.9940207

Illustrated by David Thomas Smith
Typeset in Gill Light by Midland Typesetters, Maryborough, Victoria
Printed in Australia by Australian Print Group

5 4 3 2
95 94 93 92

CONTENTS

ACKNOWLEDGEMENTS

Parts of this book have previously been published in the following magazines and newspapers:

'Translating Lonely Hearts Bullshit' appeared as 'Desperately Seeking' in *Australian Penthouse* (June '87)

'Translating Student Report Card Bullshit' appeared as 'Good one, Miss', banner article, *Daily Mirror* (11 December '87)

'Translating Job Reference Bullshit' appeared as 'Hire Intelligence' in *Australian Penthouse* (April '88)

'Translating Real Estate Ads' appeared in *Australian Penthouse* (May '88)

'Translating Doctors' Bullshit' appeared as 'Doctored English' in *Australian Penthouse* (July '88)

Many thanks to Tony Dermody, BA Dip Ed., who provided the insights for translating teachers' report cards, which led on to all the other translations, and whose idea it was to translate doctors' jargon. Special thanks to Sister Narelle Tasker, who blabbed all about doctors' jargon, despite spending the whole time saying, 'This isn't funny, I feel like I'm betraying the medical profession. Stop laughing, this isn't funny . . .' And thanks also to Jeff and Bev, who gave key insights into parent-child bullshit.

INTRODUCTORY BULLSH * T

Australians are brought up on Bullshit.

We are trained in it from an early age. As soon as we can talk we learn that telling the truth upsets people: it upsets Dad when you repeat the jokes you heard at school; it upsets Mum when you tell her about the doctors-and-nurses game you play with the kids next-door; it upsets your teachers any time you tell them anything truthful at all.

The fact is that telling the truth is impolite, but telling lies is wrong too. To solve this dilemma, Australians have invented a separate language called 'Bullshit'. Bullshit consists of English words used in such a way so as not to lie but to still encourage the listener to believe whatever fantasy they feel comfortable with.

The parent asks: 'How is my child going in school?' The teacher replies: 'He's persistent and conscientious.' (Translation: He is thick but he does his homework.)

The boss, asked for a reference, writes: 'This person has demonstrated an ability to pick up new skills.' (They can now write.) 'He takes his work very seriously.' (He's on valium.)

The dinner hostess asks: 'How did you like the meal?' The guests reply: 'Interesting.' (Awful.) 'Very unusual.' (Awful in a new and different way.)

The art of true Bullshit is to have the listener unthinkingly continue to believe whatever they want to because, if they thought at all about what was said, they would immediately say, 'Bullshit!' (thus making the correct identification).

Bullshit is all around us. It abounds in the self-references people give themselves in lonely hearts advertisements: 'disillusioned female' (my last boyfriend dumped me). It flourishes too in public political statements: 'I'll have to get back to you on that one.' (I don't understand a word you've been saying.) But Bullshit reaches its highest artistic form in real estate advertisement: 'ideal for first home owner' (made of fibro), 'handyman's delight' (the roof is about to collapse).

Welcome to the wonderful world of Australian Bullshit.

T·R·A·N·S·L·A·T·I·N·G
STUDENT REPORT CARD
BULLSH*T

Australians come into contact with Bullshit virtually from the moment they are born. When only hours old, the aunt leans over the wrinkled prune of the new baby and says, 'He has his father's looks.' (He's bald and ugly.) But the first concentrated, systematic exposure to well-meaning Bullshit is at school.

Remember that maths teacher who you used to give such a hard time to in class? And the history teacher who used to burst into tears (and you were probably partly responsible for that too)? Yet somehow, come the end of the year, your report card would emerge like a message from the netherworld, arriving in your parents' hands with glowing teachers' comments such as:

> 'Showed great application to pass this year.'
> 'A solid performance from a confident young man who is very mature for his age.'
> 'Presented a unique project.'
> 'When motivated can produce fine work.'
> 'Actively participates in class discussion.'

As any teacher will tell you, the translation of all this flowery prose into real English is: 'This kid has the academic ability of a dead wombat and the concentration span of a headless chook.'

Of course many adults, suffering from selective amnesia, remember almost nothing of their time at school and consequently have fond memories of it. These become naive parents who confront student report cards as if for the first time and face the awesome task of translating this classic Australian Bullshit into English.

The A, B, C, D, F parts, they are all pretty straightforward, but what do those spidery, hand-etched lines next to the mark mean? Of course, those are the things that prove the teacher has been coming into the classroom all year and has been attempting to pound something into the space that keeps young Johnny's ears apart, aren't they? But beyond being a vague demonstration that the teacher has probably met the child, what do they actually mean— all those 'needs to', 'appears to', 'somewhat', 'a trifle', 'a little' comments? Are they actually about your little Jilly? If so, why can't you actually understand them?

What has to be realised is that the teacher is in a classic Bullshitting situation of wanting to tell as little about the child as possible while still making a vague stab at the truth. As a guide to students, parents and would-be teachers, hereinafter are revealed the secrets of report card Bullshit.

TEACHER'S COMMENT	TRANSLATION
improved effort	passed
vastly improved effort	passed (to my surprise)
showed application to pass this year	passed (to his own surprise)
showed great application to pass this year	passed (to both our surprise)
applies herself with zest	stays awake during class
worked to capacity	thick
barely worked to capacity	can't spell her own name
shows great persistence	thick but does homework
a solid performance	pretends to do homework but doesn't
a good term's work	I don't recall this child
a fair term's work	none of the teachers recall this child
is capable of achieving an excellent report with proper motivation	a hopeless case
is not performing to his full potential	sleeps during class
gives only glimpses of his full potential	wakes up when I ask him a question
has great potential	wakes up when I ask him a question and then answers the question correctly

has some ability	which he hides well
actively participates in class discussions	will not shut up
is possessed of a vivid imagination	lies
prominent in class	sits up the back and shouts
appears to be possessed of self-doubt	refuses to answer questions in class
usually co-operative	shuts up when I tell her to
is an unpredictable student	sometimes gets the answer right
reserved	bright but socially inept
forthright	swears in class
presented a unique project	failed to answer the actual question
limited research ability	can't read
shows herself adept at practical rather than theoretical subjects	can tie her own shoelaces
calligraphy skills are excellent	forges your signature on absentee notes
needs to pay more attention in class	stares out the window all the time
cannot tolerate authority	shouts louder than I do
greater effort is needed on a more frequent basis	did homework once this term

when motivated can produce fine work	did homework twice this term
bookwork very neat	I can read her writing.
lacks listening skills	daydreams in class
reading age should improve	hoping to wean him off comics
tends to lose concentration	has an IQ of ten
has fine command of the English language	potential used car salesman
has great command of the English language	potential new car salesman
at times exhibits laziness	potential public servant
has trouble comprehending some mathematical concepts	has big future as road worker
needs to adopt a more positive attitude to herself	thinks she has the wrong answer when she has the right one; potential teacher
has limited musical ability	tone-deaf
has an inquiring mind	keeps asking me questions that I have to look up the book to answer
has a keen and inquiring mind	keeps asking me questions about my personal life
a pleasure to teach	explains the problems to me
exhibits great school spirit	hopeless at studies but does well at sport

lacks school spirit	beats up on other students at lunchtime
is a trifle emotional	bursts into tears frequently
has a disrespectful manner	threatened to bash me up
has a negative attitude	bashed me up
extremely intelligent	knows more than I do
an over-active mind	drives me bananas fidgeting all the time
well-mannered	doesn't swear in class
a confident young man	spends class time trying to chat up the female students
has had some trouble settling down into the new school	is hated by other students
has had great trouble settling down into the new school	is hated by other students and the teachers
shows great diligence as a library monitor	gets beaten up if he shows his face in the schoolyard
meticulous	a hair-splitting know-all
is popular throughout the entire school	shouts other kids cigarettes all the time
is very mature for his age	smokes marijuana
seems to lack a proper concern for the future	is on hard drugs

a somewhat shy girl	still a virgin
she is somewhat shy but making efforts to expand her range of friends	still has her virginity but is trying to lose it
a very popular young lady	the class bike
she tends to be moody	has period problems
would make a lovely mother	is pregnant
He is a keen reader.	he hides copy of *Penthouse* inside school text
He is a very keen reader.	actually reads the articles in *Penthouse*
He strongly favours the biological sciences.	keeps looking up girls' dresses
She tends to have trouble settling down each day.	I thinks she's pregnant and has morning sickness.
takes a keen interest in other students' work	copies homework from other kids
rarely brings proper equipment to class	has sold all her schoolbooks to buy cigarettes
has a good sense of line and proportion	doodles in class
could take more care with his personal appearance	washes once a month
needs to improve personal hygiene	not toilet-trained

has written about some interesting ideas	has lurid sexual fantasies
an interesting literary style	writes obscene short stories; has great future as journalist
strong leadership qualities	a gang leader
achieved a few breathtaking moments	farts in class
I find this child upsets me.	I am having marital problems.
This result does not truly reflect your child's ability.	I'm a terrible teacher.
may do better in a more academically orientated school	This is a terrible school.
may do better in a less academically orientated school	potential process worker
Your child is a credit to the family and the school.	We know you have lots of money and could you please make a large donation to the school?

So you've made it out of school with a C in maths, a B in history and an A in garbage detail. But did you learn anything useful? Did the school equip you for a job? More importantly, did it give you a mastery of Australian Bullshit so that you can write extremely impressive job applications that don't actually say anything? For it is when you have to find a job or change jobs that you again unavoidably encounter the challenge of using and translating Australian Bullshit.

T·R·A·N·S·L·A·T·I·N·G
JOB REFERENCE
BULLSH * T

There are many times in life when one does not say exactly what one thinks. In fact, that last sentence was one of them. Because the truth is that there are not many times in life that one *does* say exactly what one thinks. There are libel and slander laws to stop that sort of thing.

This is complicated when you are supposed to write down what you think about another person. This is called 'giving a job reference' and the main object of this is to make the person sound so good that they will get the new job and not come back and pester you to write another reference for them. Even more important is to ensure that this turkey will work somewhere else and not come back to work for you.

This means that the prospective employer is faced with a decoding problem. Could this anaemic, trembling social leper stuttering his way through the interview be the same superman described as:

> *A diligent worker with an enormous capacity for following orders. An enthusiastic, organised, efficient and punctual employee who, in a short time, quickly made himself indispensable. Patient and persistent, he has a demonstrated ability to pick up new skills. Nothing was too difficult for him. This is a person who takes his work very seriously and is adept at handling awkward inquiries. I would not hesitate to recommend this person to any prospective employer.*

All of which translates as: 'This person is a pathetic wimp.'

It is all very obvious once you have mastered the secret language of job references.

PREVIOUS EMPLOYER'S COMMENT	TRANSLATION
diligent	always checks and double-checks the accuracy of his pay cheque
has an enormous capacity for following orders	cannot think for himself
enthusiastic	only takes an hour for lunch

organised, efficient	has a neat desk
punctual	only arrives ten minutes late for work
punctual and diligent	only arrives five minutes late for work
in a short time, quickly made himself indispensable	re-organised the filing system so that nobody else could understand it
patient and persistent	slow
has demonstrated an ability to pick up new skills	can now write
nothing was too difficult for him	*nothing* was too difficult for him
takes his work very seriously	is on valium
adept at handling awkward inquiries	knows how to put the telephone on hold
shows personal initiative	helps herself to office stationery
shows a willingness to work erratic hours	never shows up to work on time
ambitious	keeps asking for pay rises
attacks every task with a highly professional attitude	will not do a scrap of work that he is not paid for
relaxed person who can cope with pressure	dozes off in the afternoon
energetic	does not doze off in the afternoon

has shown herself keen to take on new responsibilities	gets bored easily
tactful and considerate	lies
adept at handling difficult clients	not ashamed to grovel
has shown that she knows the value of hard work	only works when she thinks she is being watched
a natural leader who inspires loyalty in others	leads the charge to the pub on Friday nights
works well under pressure	works only when under pressure
has demonstrated an ability to delegate responsibility	passes the buck
worked well under difficult conditions	was hated by the other employees
has an acute grasp of the workings of committees	stabs people in the back
I have seen her develop into an efficient worker.	She can now do the job without tripping over herself.
will go far	goes too far
a person of strong character	knows how to say 'no' with authority
tireless	worked through lunch once
able to keep his finger on the pulse	unable to keep his fingers off the secretaries
a lively personality	will not shut up

has demonstrated admirable research skills	reads the newspaper everyday
She related particularly well to other women members of the team.	I think she's a lesbian.
forward-thinking	asks too many questions
an open, forthright personality	swears all the time
able to make quick decisions	able to make hasty decisions
able to devise a plan and see it carried through	was responsible for the tea roster
has shown an ability for conceptual thought	daydreams all the time
has impressed all with his friendly attitude	sleeps around
Although she only worked for us for a short time, she impressed all who came into contact with her.	I have never met this person.
has a marked ability to work alone	cannot get along with other people
can look forward to a brighter future	as his past is so dismal
Her good nature made her a joy to work with.	She smiles inanely all the time.
I personally will be sorry to see him leave.	He owes me money.

I cannot recommend him strongly enough.	We drink together.
has shown a willingness to work long hours	has shown a willingness to collect overtime payments
displayed great strength of personality	regularly disobeyed orders
a likeable young man	an idiot
a personable young man	an idiot who wears a tie
developed original projects	developed disasters
shows management potential	likes to sit and watch other people working
has an ability to turn her hand to many different tasks	cannot concentrate on one thing for more than five minutes
a regular, reliable person	goes to the toilet every day at the same time
bubbly personality	an alcoholic
thrives on challenges	tried to tidy up the office storeroom
I only ever have to tell her something once.	and then she repeats it to every bloody person in the place
fastidious in her work	points out my mistakes—the little pest
extraordinarily gifted	able to organise a filing system
a pleasure to work with	is cheerful in the morning

dedicated	does not leave work until five o'clock
an open, friendly disposition	sexually active
extraordinarily popular	the local marijuana supplier
a high level of personal organisation	owns a diary
gifted at long-range planning	keeps talking about what he is going to do when he retires
capable of growing into any job	capable of learning office secrets
a young person who knows where he is going	he is going out of this office and is *never coming back*
talented	passed her HSC
has drawn the admiration of her workmates	she wears expensive clothes
has drawn the admiration of his workmates	has a great-looking girlfriend
a wonderful sense of tact	lies to the boss about how she looks
a quiet, steady temperament	is always depressed
a lively sense of humour	tells crude jokes instead of working
capable of anything	capable of absolutely *anything*
honest	has not been to prison (as far as I know)

honest and trustworthy	is the only person in the office who does not steal the office stationery
self-confident	was after my job, the little twerp
is able to advise with policy decisions at the highest level	is a know-all
has displayed a high degree of competence	can spell
shows great determination to achieve what she wants	nags
persistent	thick
persistent and conscientious	thick but tries hard
the sort of person you can turn to in a crisis	because she is the one who will have started it
I would not hesitate to recommend this person to any prospective employer.	This person has so little character they would fit in anywhere.

All right, you've finally got yourself a decent job (translation: a job where you're paid more than you're worth). But now you've got it, the trouble is getting to it. So with visions in your head of cruising around town, attracting the eye of the opposite sex and the envy of the same sex, you start your search for a freedom machine: A CAR OF YOUR OWN.

T·R·A·N·S·L·A·T·I·N·G
USED CAR
BULLSH*T

The only thing you can be sure of with a used car is that somebody else doesn't want it. Isn't this telling you something?

Immaculate. Genuine one-owner.
First to see will buy. Must sell.
Fun car. Reliable. Superb runabout.
Bargain. Extractors. Air. Many
extras. $9,000 o.n.o.

How could anyone ever bear to part with such a magnificent vehicle? You feel like a heel for even thinking of taking it away from him, the poor guy.

Until a few months later, as you are parked on the side of the road waiting for the tow truck, you begin to radically revise your opinion of the man's character.

It could all have been avoided if only you'd studied how to translate used car Bullshit.

WHAT THE AD SAYS	TRANSLATION
Valiant	what you have to be to buy this car
only one previous owner	a demolition derby driver
a classic car	an incredibly old car
excellent condition	You won't find any rust—it's there but you won't find it.
good condition	You will find some rust.
fair condition	You will find some parts unrusted.
needs some work	needs towing
two-tone	two-tone: blue and rust
goes well	downhill

goes very well	no brakes
panel van	stained rear carpet
ideal second car	ideal for spare parts
demo model	demolition model
prestige auto	impossible to get spare parts for
12 months' rego	I'm selling it now while I've got my best chance of unloading this heap.
fun car	fun if you like working on cars
first to see will buy	as long as they don't try driving it
unreg	unregisterable (ever)
s/roof	a hole in the roof
bargain	what a potential buyer would be well-advised to do
must sell	This car has driven me to bankruptcy.
many extras	four hub-caps
reluctantly sold because owner is moving	stolen
extractors	what the seller is trying to do to your wallet
great	the sound the gear change makes

new tyres	cheap retreads
reconditioned motor	second-hand
alarm	what you will feel soon after you buy this car
mech A1	mechanically, a one that you will need to have examined professionally
p/steer	when you turn the steering wheel, the tyres at the front move
rad/cass	something used to cover up the knocking noises coming from the engine
cent. lock	when you turn the door key, the doors lock
mag wheels	no hub-caps
urgent sale	I can't afford the repayments.
log books	something to read while you're waiting for the tow truck
4 wheel discs	has brakes
immaculate	a virgin; never used for sex
as new	mechanically hopeless but duco looks good
tow bar	engine is clapped out from hauling boats
superb runabout	what the seller is giving the buyer

no rust	only extremely gullible buyers should inspect
hatch	has rear door
always garaged	We were too ashamed to park this car out the front of the house.
air-con.	con
nothing to spend	what the current owner has left after getting it fixed up
station wagon	good when stationary
ute	no rear seat
previously owned by little old lady	who burnt the clutch out
reliable	slow
solid, reliable	very slow
ideal lady's car	already dented

Now you have your job (or, as you fondly call it, 'hell') and your car (or, as you fondly know it, 'the money guzzler'). But still there is something missing from your life: a spouse, a partner, the other half, the significant other. So, after work, you get in your car and head off to parties, dances or bars, in the endless quest for Miss Right or Mr Right or Person Right . . .

T·R·A·N·S·L·A·T·I·N·G
BOY–GIRL
BULLSH*T

AFTER TWO YEARS OF DATING, OVERNIGHTS, ARGUMENTS, TRIAL SEPARATION, RECONCILIATIONS AND COUNSELLING, DAVID AND I HAVE FINALLY AGREED THAT WE WANT THE SAME THING...

D.T.S.

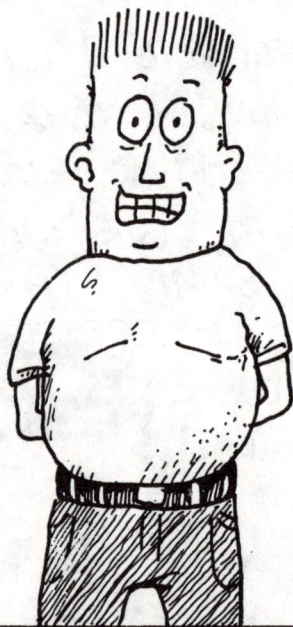

What's the difference between a good relationship and a bad relationship?

About four months.

But it can seem a lot longer.

Words are a problem. You may think you have trouble explaining what sort of cut you want from the butcher, but that's nothing like the problem of trying to explain what sort of cut you want from your partner.

The trouble is that men and women can use the same words to mean absolutely different things. If she says, 'I love you', it usually means, 'When are we going to move in together?' If he says, 'Of course I love you', it usually means, 'Don't bother me, I'm watching TV.'

That instant when Boy meets Girl is so often a magic moment: Boy's eyes meet Girl's eyes across a crowded, smoke-filled room . . . But then mouths open and things start to get complicated. Let us follow these oral outpourings of Boy and Girl and see what they really mean.

The first meeting, at a reasonably good party . . .

WHAT THEY SAY

WHAT THEY MEAN

WHAT THEY SAY	WHAT THEY MEAN
Man: What do you do for a living?	I'm a hip, non-sexist guy who accepts the fact that women work—can I jump you?
Girl: I'm a nurse.	I'm used to handling bodies.
Man: Really?	This is my lucky night.
Girl: What do you normally do on weekends?	Do you have a girlfriend?
Man: I go to a lot of parties.	I like to fool around.
Man: How do you keep so fit?	How did you get that great body?

Girl: Aerobics.	I like sex.
Man: There's a film on at the drive-in that I really want to see.	I want to fondle your breasts.
Girl: I haven't been to a drive-in for ages.	I haven't had sex in a car for ages.
Man: Can I give you a ride home?	Can I ride you?

Later the same night, the man pulls his car up outside her flat . . .

Man: Can I walk you to the door?	Can I put my tongue inside your mouth?
Girl: This is a bad time for me.	I've got my period.
Man: Oh, what's wrong?	I'll pretend I'm sympathetic if that will help me get into your pants.
Girl: I've just been through a bad time.	I just split up with a louse.
Man: Oh . . .	Oh god, another woman with hang-ups.
Girl: I don't think I'm ready for anything too heavy.	I'm not ready for sex.
Man: It's no big deal.	Aaaaaah! (Maybe I should hurry back to the party and see what other women are still there.)
Girl: Would you like to come in for a quick cup of coffee?	On the other hand, I might like your hands all over me.
Man: Yeah, sure.	I'm going to sco-ore.
Girl: Just for a while.	Don't get too cocky.

28

Man: Yep.	I wish this girl would make her bloody mind up.

A few minutes later, inside her flat . . .

Girl: You're an interesting person.	I think I want you inside me but I'm not quite sure.
Man: Well, I think you're a very interesting person too.	Your body interests me.
Girl: We look nice together.	I hope you're seeing this as more than just a one-night stand.
Man: Yeah.	It's time to stop talking and start doing.
Girl: I think you're the sort of person I'd like to get to know better.	I definitely want you inside me.

Cupid runs amok but, as so often happens, this fickle dwarf only shoots one of the partners. So that after a few months, weeks, days or perhaps even just hours, the relationship has become divided into the keen and the nowhere-near-as-keen . . .

WHAT THE KEEN ONE SAYS	WHAT IT MEANS
You can leave a few of your things here if you like.	Start thinking in terms of years.
I can't believe how lucky we are to have found each other.	You're never going to get rid of me.
What does our relationship mean to you?	Are you going to be faithful to me?
I need you.	I have psychological problems.

29

I'll never find another person like you.

If you ever leave me, I'll kill myself.

We've known each other for over six months now.

It's time we moved in together.

We've known each other for over a year now.

It's time we bought a house together.

We've known each other for almost two years now.

When the hell are you going to marry me?

I'm not getting any younger.

I want children *now*.

I think we should stop mucking around.

If you don't get serious, we really will stop mucking around.

WHAT THE NOT-SO-KEEN ONE IS LIKELY TO SAY

TRANSLATION

Where are my socks?

Please don't tell me you love me. I can't handle being loved.

Can we talk about this later? I'm in a bit of a rush.

I can't handle commitment.

I like you. I really like you.

I'm not in love with you.

No, I really value our relationship. I really value what we have now.

I don't want to get married, and I don't want to change it into anything else more serious.

The world turns, the days of our lives mount up, and the bold and the beautiful are young and becoming increasingly restless.

Girl: I wish you'd grow up.

You know all those things you do that I used to think were really cute? Well, now they drive me bananas.

Man: I was only looking at the woman.

Don't interrupt me, I'm having a fantasy.

Girl: Do you still love me?

Are you porking someone else on the side?

Man: Of course I still love you.

I used to love you.

Man: You always seem to be tense nowadays.

You never want sex.

Girl: You can't expect it to be as good as it was in the first few weeks.

I don't want to screw you any more.

Man: We do seem to have got ourselves into a bit of a rut.

Do you remember what head jobs are?

Girl: Well, you're always in such a rush lately.

Do you remember what foreplay is?

Man: I've got a lot of things on my mind at the moment.

I've got a lot of things on my mind at the moment—and you're not one of them.

Girl: We don't do things together any more.

The only time I come is when you're not there.

Man: We're always doing what you want to do.

We're always sleeping instead of fooling around.

Girl: There are more things in life than sex, you know.

I don't want to boink you any more.

Man: I know that.

There's also arguing, which is what we seem to do all the time.

Girl: You never seem to listen to what I say.

I never listen to what you say, I assume you do the same thing.

Man: Things aren't the way they used to be.

You make me want to vomit.

Girl: You don't take me seriously.

You take me—not very often mind you—but when you do take me you're pretty casual about it.

Man: Well, you don't take all the things I do seriously.

I was serious about that vibrator.

Girl: We always do what you want to.

You're always making sexual demands on me that I give in to, even though I don't really feel like it.

Man: When?

When?

Girl: You just don't understand.

You're a mental pygmy.

Man: Remember when we used to have such great times?

I'm bored.

Girl: We've stopped growing as people.

You're holding me back in life.

Man: We don't talk like we used to.

We don't do anything like we used to.

Girl: We can work this out.

We can't possibly work this out but I want to appear to be the more reasonable one.

Man: Maybe we need a break from each other.

I want to move out.

Girl: Maybe you're right—just until we sort ourselves out.

Hooray! Hooray! Hooray!

Eventually you despair of the party-and-pub rat-race and instead seek your one and only true love through a more modern means: mass media.

T·R·A·N·S·L·A·T·I·N·G
LONELY HEARTS
BULLSH * T

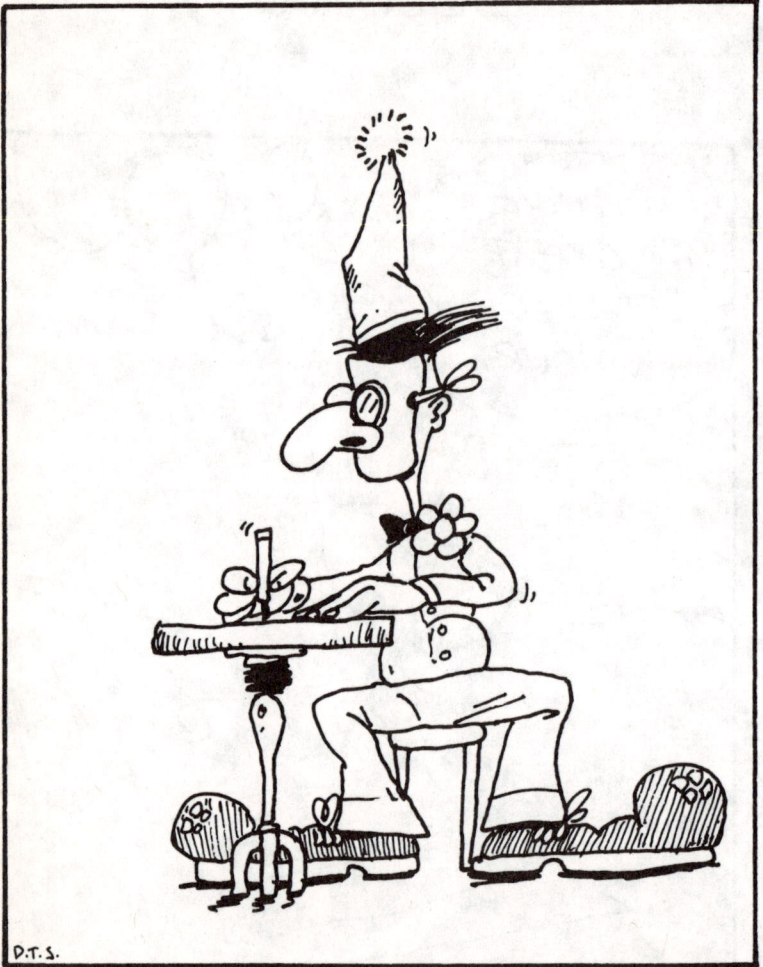

There is an old saying among nudists: 'It pays to advertise.'

But many single people feel that there must be a less graphic way to accomplish self-advertisement. This more obscure, more tasteful and slightly less embarrassing method is via lonely hearts advertisements. This practice has become so startlingly popular that many universities are poised to introduce degree courses analysing its content and style.

Every day, hundreds of brave Australians sit down and try to encapsulate their whole lives plus what they are looking for in a partner in twenty words or less—or more, if you can afford the extra charges.

And every day thousands—well, hundreds—well, dozens—of members of the opposite sex—or possibly the same sex in certain parts of Sydney—sit down and try to decipher these cryptic telegrams from the heart and see if any tug at the strings of their own heart—or possibly some other organ.

But how are they to decode cryptic messages like:

Hi. 25yo. 5'6 tall. Outgoing,
shy, retiring, reserved,
independent, refined, feminine,
hopelessly romantic, disillusioned
Aries with bubbly personality
looking for kind, considerate,
loving man who is financially
secure and seeking a steady
relationship. Me: tertiary
educated, average weight and will
try anything once. You: someone
who knows how to pamper and
protect. Personality is more
important than looks.

What's it all mean? Is this the sort of woman you want to spend your life with? Is this the sort of woman you would want to spend the night with? Is this the sort of woman on whom you would want to spend the four dollars it costs to reply to the ad? Indeed, is this a woman?

LADIES

WHAT SHE SAYS ABOUT HERSELF	TRANSLATION
quiet and reserved	I won't go to bed on the first date.
friendly but quiet type	I won't go to bed on the first date but will think about it a lot.
Christian	I won't do anything below the waist until we're engaged.
looking for friendship and fun	First, we'll become friends and then we'll start to have some *real* fun.
disillusioned female	My last boyfriend dumped me.
great sense of humour	I dumped my last boyfriend.
easygoing	I won't mind if you make a pass at me on the first date because I have learnt how to turn men down while smiling.
warm and sensuous	I like to use my tongue a lot when kissing.
fun to be with	I like sex.
independent	I won't blame you if I don't have an orgasm.
can cope with most situations	I don't mind if you live with your mother.
feminine	I shave my underarms.

sexy	I shave my underarms and my legs.
witty	I'll make fun of your sexual hang-ups.
interests are many and varied	I read Barbara Cartland novels.
I enjoy dining out.	I can't cook.
refined	I use nail polish.
adventurous	I once went camping.
spunky	I dye my hair blonde.
strong personality	I like to get on top.
forceful personality	I don't care whether or not you have an orgasm.
very forceful personality	I rape men at knifepoint.
bubbly personality	I talk non-stop.
I admire integrity.	I don't fake orgasms.
will try anything once	have tried everything many times
average weight	desperate to lose a couple of kilos
tertiary-educated	I was sexually deprived during high school and have been trying to make up for it ever since.
well-spoken	I sell Amway.
I love life.	I love shopping.

I have a heart as big as myself.	I give at doorknock appeals.
no ties	I don't own my own home.
financially secure	I got a great divorce settlement.
I like discos.	I have herpes.
home-loving	I'm in love with my furniture.
well-travelled	I've been around.
cosmopolitan	I once had an Italian boyfriend.
articulate	I know how to say 'no' and make you believe I mean it.
I'm told I'm beautiful.	but I don't believe it myself
down to earth	I talk openly about my period pains.
looking for a serious relationship	I want to live with a man.
seeking meaningful relationship	I want to get married.
looking for a permanent partner	I want to have kids.
one in a million	I have multiple orgasms easily.
liberated woman	I don't shave my legs.
very fit and active	I do aerobics classes.
fit and active	I play tennis.
fit	I make the bed every day.

open-minded	I will try out new sexual positions.
still single	I want to get married before I turn into an old maid.
romantic	I like to kiss before getting it on.
hopeless romantic	I won't go to bed until I start falling in love with you but don't worry because this usually only takes fifteen minutes.
completely hopeless romantic	If you try to leave me, I will kill myself.

WHAT SHE SAYS SHE IS LOOKING FOR

TRANSLATION

seeking someone who is sincere and genuine	I want to get married.
genuine and sincere; gentlemen only need apply	My last boyfriend cheated on me.
looking for sensitive, caring male	I want a man who gives long foreplay.
looking for kind, considerate, loving man	I want a man who gives very long foreplay.
looking for man with old-world values	I won't go to bed until you've proposed marriage.
looking for well-groomed man	I want to marry a white-collar worker.

personality is more important than looks	I'm ugly.
I am seeking someone for companionship.	I don't like sex.
want male who is financially secure	I have money and want to avoid gold-diggers.
seeking steady relationship	Look, we both know it probably won't last forever but let's be faithful to each other while it does.
I want the simple things in life.	I want a house in an upper-class suburb with a swimming pool and a Volvo station wagon.
looking for sensitive man	looking for someone to share the housework
no ocker types	I insist on a fair amount of foreplay.
I want a man without hang-ups	I don't do kinky sex.
I want a man who knows how to pamper and protect	I'm looking for a father figure.
all letters faithfully answered	first ten letters faithfully answered

GENTS

WHAT HE SAYS ABOUT HIMSELF	TRANSLATION
quiet and reserved	I am terrible in bed.

friendly but quiet type	I like to be seduced.
Christian	I won't do it on the first date.
looking for friendship and fun	looking to get laid
disillusioned male	My alimony payments are killing me.
irreverant sense of humour	I fart in bed.
easygoing	I won't mind if we don't go to bed on the first date.
warm and sensitive	I like to use my tongue during sex.
fun-loving	I like to hold women down and tickle them until they throw up.
independent	I have lots of money.
can cope with most situations	I don't mind if you've got herpes.
unselfish	I will try to hold back until you've had your orgasm.
masculine	I have a hairy chest.
sexy	I have hairy legs.
charming	I'm overweight but I talk well.
interests are many and varied	I play squash.
I enjoy dining out or dining in.	I eat.

refined	I studied French at high school.
adventurous	I am prepared to risk not using a condom.
spunky	I dye my hair blond.
strong personality	I don't bother with foreplay.
forceful personality	I insist on going to bed on the first date.
very forceful personality	I like to spank women.
I admire integrity	If I cheat on you, I'll tell you about it in graphic detail.
will try anything once	I like the idea of anal intercourse.
average weight	no muscles
tertiary-educated	I like to be walked over by women wearing high heels.
well-spoken	I'm a used car salesman.
I love life.	I love sex.
I have a heart as big as myself.	I'm a dwarf.
no ties	I wear cravats
well-mannered	I apologise if I ejaculate prematurely.
well-situated	I own my own home.
financially secure	I have a boring job.

I like discos.	Basically, I am a shallow person but I have a lot of energy.
I like videos.	Basically, I am a shallow person and I don't have much energy.
I enjoy good conversations.	as these are rare when I'm around
well-travelled	I've been on a singles cruise.
cosmopolitan	I've been to New Zealand.
articulate	I think I can talk you into bed, or bore you into it anyway.
I'm told I'm good-looking.	by my mother
down to earth	I only know two sexual positions.
looking for serious relationship	looking for relationship that will last over a month
seeking meaningful relationship	looking for relationship that will last two months
looking for a partner	looking for a relationship that will last six months
one in a million	I'm a virgin.
I believe in women's rights	I expect to go dutch everywhere.
very fit and active	I'm in my 30s.
fit and active	I'm in my 40s.
fit	I'm in my 50s.

open-minded	I like oral sex.
still very single	I'm not interested in marriage.
romantic	I like to have dinner with a woman before getting it on.
hopeless romantic	I can remember the names of my previous girlfriends.
completely hopeless romantic	I cried when I saw *Love Story*.

WHAT HE SAYS HE IS LOOKING FOR	TRANSLATION
she must love to have good times	I want someone who will do it on the first date.
looking for well-presented lady.	I don't want anyone with herpes.
looking for that special lady	Ugly ladies need not apply.
looking for lady with a great sense of humour	because you'll need it when you see me in the nude
Give me a try.	I'm desperate.
all letters faithfully answered	I expect to get two replies.

Eventually you find your perfect partner. You even take the marriage or cohabitation plunge and so the two of you begin to search for that special place to call your own. And now you're really in trouble.

T·R·A·N·S·L·A·T·I·N·G
REAL ESTATE AD
BULLSH * T

The first problem facing a home buyer (otherwise known as the mortgagee) is money. But the second problem is learning to speak a new language. That new language is the language of real estate advertisements. This second problem is liable to be bigger than the first.

There are three kinds of falsehoods: lies, damn lies and real estate ads. Real estate ads, of course, never lie. Rather, they are a form of poetry and poetry does not lie. However, it doesn't exactly tell the truth either. Rather, poetry uses language in new and inventive ways to convey an image pleasing to the reader; similarly, real estate ads.

> *Neat cottage. Ideal holiday home or for*
> *first home owner. Partially renovated.*
> *Quiet street. Excellent investment*
> *opportunity. Will not last at this*
> *price. Forced sale.*

Doesn't this cast up images of rustic charm? A little solid brick bungalow surrounded with greenery. However, the translation of this into real English is: *small, old fibro home about to fall down.*

It is all very obvious once you learn to understand the poetic licence of real estate ads.

WHAT THE AD SAYS	TRANSLATION
three-bedroom	two bedrooms and a large cupboard with a window
spacious	four bedrooms
neat	two bedrooms
tasteful	carpeted
leafy aspects	trees block out your view
magnificent aspects	on hill
close to public transport	underneath railway line

47

brand new	one year old
new	three years old
as new	six years old
modern	ten years old
solid	fifteen years old
cottage	twenty-five years old
full of character	fifty years old
developers take note	the house is falling down
handyman's delight	the roof is about to collapse
investment opportunity	needs a lot of money spent on it
absolute waterfrontage	prone to flooding
quiet street	everyone else got smart and moved out
ideal for first home owner	fibro
warm, rustic feel	wooden
magnificent	brick
easy walking distance to	five kilometres away from
executive-style living	has a spa
beautifully presented	the lawn has been mown
well-presented	is for sale

REAL ESTATE AD BULLSH*T

low maintenance	aluminium windows
en suite	toilet flushes will wake you up in the middle of the night
short walk to shops	five minute walk to shops
minutes to shops	ten minute walk to shops
handy to shops	nowhere near shops
immaculate home	vacuumed
delightful cottage	overgrown garden
will not last at this price	will not sell for this price
enormous potential	enormous amount of work to do
nothing to spend	after buying this you'll have nothing left to spend
lovely brick veneer	built in the '60s
prime location	next to factory
inner city living at its best	close to muggers
close to school	close to vandals
cathedral ceilings	you will need to pray a lot
partially renovated	owner gave up on this hopeless case
open fire	black ceilings
retirement special	a good home to die in

the entertainer	has lounge room
park-like rear garden	full of dog shit
situated in rapidly progressing area	in the back blocks
potential value is immeasurable	present value is minimal
a rare find	rare to find a house made like this still standing
rarely does one find that slightly different home	converted funeral parlour
above-ground pool	piece of leaky plastic filled with water
forced sale	owner committed suicide
sought-after location	frequently broken into
close to amenities	next to public toilets
not much to mow	no land
generous built-ins	has cupboards
older-style home	outside toilet only
contemporary split-level dwelling	overpriced
needs some TLC	white ants
suitable for pole home	on cliff
modern kitchen	has taps

REAL ESTATE AD BULLSH*T

suit young family	can allow kids to run riot; nothing worth preserving from damage
fully landscaped grounds	has garden
outdoor entertainment area	barbeque
ideal holiday home	uncarpeted
unique home	mud brick
prestige surrounds	all the other houses in the street are nicer
loads of character	bizarre
includes all the things that make a house a home	has indoor toilet

At last you have settled into your dream home (well, it gives the bank manager nice dreams) and the two of you decide to take the ultimate plunge: you decide to bring another human life into this world. Congratulations, it's a healthy, blue-eyed tax deduction.

T·R·A·N·S·L·A·T·I·N·G
PARENT-CHILD
BULLSH*T

As every mother knows, childbirth is not the hardest thing in the world; stopping yourself from wringing the kids' necks is the hardest thing in the world.

When they are born, you silently promise yourself that you are never ever going to say the things to your child that you so much hated your parents saying to you. But, horror of horrors, after only a few years you find yourself using the exact same phrases on your young terrors.

'Don't you want to help me?' Remember how much you hated your mother saying that to you? Yuk. 'Don't talk back to your mother.'—another one you really hated; why didn't they ever allow you to express yourself? 'Because I say so, that's why.' Why couldn't they take the time to explain it to you?

But there you are, using the same phrases on your children. And, guess what, they feel just the same way about hearing these phrases that you did. There is only one thing worse than being a parent, and that's being the child of a parent.

Eventually you come to realise that all you are doing is unconsciously copying your mother or your father's way of talking to children because that is the only way you ever learnt to talk to children. So you may decide to do Parent Effectiveness Training. This helps you a lot. You still shout at the kids but you do it in a much more effective way.

WHAT THE PARENT SAYS — TRANSLATION

WHAT THE PARENT SAYS	TRANSLATION
Ask your father.	It's your father's turn to say no.
Ask your mother.	I'm too tired to say no.
Can't you see Mummy is busy at the moment?	Rack off.
Why don't you just go and play outside for a while?	If you don't get out of here, I'll rip your lungs out.
. . . else.	the terrifying alternative to doing what you're told

What did you do?	What did you break?
What happened?	How did you hurt your sister?
pee-pee	the male sexual organ
whizz	urination
potty	what parents go when trying to train their child to use this
I will count to three . . .	On the count of three I will turn into a dragon . . .
one . . .	see my nostrils flare
two . . .	see fire coming out of my mouth
three . . .	see these talons
that's it . . .	see what these talons can do
Whatever you're doing, stop it.	all-purpose order to kids who you can hear having fun but can't see
Because I said so, and that's good enough.	Parents rule, okay.
Shut up.	Please keep quiet.
Would you *please* keep quiet?	I am trying not to shout at you. Be warned.
For God's sake, will you shut up.	Shut up or risk meeting God first-hand.
Go to your bedroom and be quiet.	I can't stand this noise any more.
What *are* you doing?	Why are you creating this mess?
Isn't it past your bedtime?	It is past your bedtime.

Get to bed this instant.	I am very concerned that you should get sufficient quiet rest in your life and if you don't go and get some quiet rest right now, I'll beat the hell out of you.
because	the all-purpose answer to 'Why?'
because because	the all-purpose answer to 'Why because?'
I haven't got time to explain it to you now.	No good reason.
Have you ever tried it?	Ridiculous meal-time question number one. Unless the child has been dashing up to the supermarket and surreptitiously cooking gourmet meals behind your back, you know he hasn't tried it.
How do you know you won't like it until you've tried it?	Ridiculous meal-time question number two. By this reasoning the parent should try eating cow manure, raw beetles and rotten eggs.
Eat everything and you'll get some ice-cream.	I am training you to be a sugar addict.
Yes, you have to eat it.	I know it tastes pretty ordinary but the diet books say it's good for you.
It's that or nothing.	Not much of a choice really, is it?
All right then, starve to death.	I am training you to become anorexic.

56

soon

when car trips always come to an end

What the hell did you do?

How did you mess up your nice clean clothes so quickly?

I'm sick of telling you.

If I have to tell you again, it will be your turn to feel sick.

Who started it?

Who do I hit?

I don't care.

Cut the long explanation and just tell me who hit whom first.

What did you do to her?

How did you hurt her and with what?

Come here!

You are about to be hit.

Put some clothes on.

Stop running around the house holding your penis.

in a minute

never

Wait until I'm finished what I'm doing.

Go away.

Aaaaaaaaaaaaaaaaaaaaah!

Oh dear, the children are bothering me a little at the moment.

Stop whingeing.

I want to whinge about the fact that you whinge all the time— you don't hear me whingeing do you?

I'm not going to do it if you whinge!

If you stop whingeing, I'll forget to do it.

You're gonna be in big trouble if you don't stop that.

I have no idea what I'm going to do to you if you don't stop it.

Right, you're in big trouble now, mister.

Right, I'm in big trouble because now I have to think up what 'big trouble' means.

Because I say so, that's why.

Because I spank harder than you, that's why.

Don't you want to help me?

I want you to prove you love me by enjoying doing things you hate doing.

Don't argue with your mother.

Don't copy your father.

Don't be so childish.

!!!

Act your age!

Act four years old?

Get to your room!

Save yourself from my anger.

Go to sleep!

Pretend to be asleep!

Tidy up your room!

I am sick of your room being a reflection of how I feel inside.

Or . . .

The terrible, nameless thing parents threaten to do to children. 'Do this or . . .' This seems to work as it fills the child with or.

Just you wait until your father gets home.

Your father is a psychopath.

Just you wait until your mother gets home.

Your mother terrifies me. I assume she has the same effect on you.

You're making me very angry.

I'm making me very angry but I'd rather blame you.

If you don't stop crying, I'll hit you.

I can't handle it when you cry.

Anybody would think that
you didn't love me.

This is your weekly training in
guilt.

You know I only work such
long hours for you kids.

It's your fault I have to work
so hard.

They're your children you
know.

Except if we get divorced, in
which case they're my children.

Do what you're told, for
Christ's sake.

You're mother is in an impossible
mood. Tread carefully. I am.

Of course I love my kids.

I just happen to intensely resent
them at the moment.

I wish you'd grow up.

I wish you'd act more mature and
responsible than I do.

All right then, we'll go
without you.

Would you *please get ready!*

All right then, we won't go.

I don't care that you don't want
to go, we're going and you're
coming too.

We only do this for your
own good.

We only do this for a bit of
peace and quiet.

Do you know what the word
'exasperating' means?

Are you a precocious genius?

Not bad.

Excellent, outstanding, wonderful, brilliant, that's the best you've
ever done, just superb, you're so
wonderful.

WHAT THE CHILD SAYS

TRANSLATION

Do I have to?

I know I have to but I don't have
to like it.

Mum-can-I . . .

Mum

Dad-can-I . . .

Mum won't let me.

Mum said I could.

Mum said to ask you.

Da-a-a-a-d, can I . . .

Mum would say no if I asked her but if you say yes, she'll be too embarrassed to say no.

Why can't I watch TV when I want to?

Why can't I be like Dad?

They'll be sorry when I'm dead.

I'll watch all the TV I want when I'm dead.

Why?

I know you won't tell me why but I want to annoy you to get my own back.

Ohhhhhhhhhhhh.

I wish I could but you won't let me so I'm going to make this horrible grating noise to annoy you.

Excuse me . . .

I know I'm interrupting but I'm doing it in such a cutsey way that you can't possibly not give me some attention.

No.

I want to see how much I can get away with, without being hit.

Please?

This is my last resort.

She did it.

Hit her not me.

I wasn't doing anything.

I wasn't doing anything you'd like.

I don't wanna.

No, thank you, if it's all the same to you, I would rather not.

It was her.	I didn't break it.
nothing	what children are always doing at the time one of their siblings bursts into tears
He fell down.	all-purpose answer to 'Why is your brother crying?'
Daddy, Daddy, Daddy . . .	My brother has been hitting me.
He bumped his head.	My brother deliberately rammed his face into my fist.
I won't be your friend any more.	I want to be in charge.
Ohhh, yuk, this is horrible . . .	This dish, while not without merit, is not to my particular taste.
now	when I expect all my wants in life met
When are we gonna be there?	Oh dear, the car has just pulled out of the driveway.
I'm bored.	Can we play that game where everything you suggest, I turn my nose up at?
She hit me first.	which therefore justifies my subsequent maiming and torture of her

Finally, life is as it should be: you have a spouse, two kids, a dog, a barbeque and a mortgage. Now you can relax, knowing that our wise and sage politicians are looking after our country, the economy and interest rates. If you don't believe me, just ask them.

WHAT THE POLITICIAN SAYS	TRANSLATION
I am shocked to find out that such things have been going on.	I am shocked to find out that such things have been discovered by the press.
The honourable member's memory seems to be faulty.	He's a bloody liar.
we in the government	I
responsible government involves	getting re-elected involves
I have faith in the Australian public.	I have faith in my publicity machine.
There is no need to panic.	There is a need to think about moving overseas.
scumbags	the honourable members of the opposition
The press has to show a greater sense of responsibility.	We need someone to set us an example.
We can look forward in the long term to a better economic climate.	We can look forward to short-term bankruptcy.
broadening the tax base	inventing new forms of taxation
tax relief	indirect taxes
I will not be calling an early election.	I'm not saying when the early election is.
a waste of public funds	how the opposition wants to spend your money

government projects	how we want to spend your money
necessary cuts	politically acceptable cuts
overseas jaunts	trips taken by members of other parties
overseas visits	trips taken by members of my party
election promises	promises we may elect to keep or we may not
a difficult decision	a decision that may cost us votes
This decision was one we have decided to reconsider.	This decision was one that would have cost us too many votes.
I don't pay any attention to polls.	The polls are against me.
As you know I'm a poll-follower.	I'm ahead in the polls.
I can sense the mood of the electorate.	The polls are wrong.
a vocal minority	people who disagree with me
the majority of sensible Australians	people who agree with me
I believe in democracy.	I believe that right-thinking people agree with me and wrong-thinking people (those who do not agree with me) are communists.

I haven't had a chance to look into it.	I have been busy on my boat.
The decision isn't really up to me.	I'm passing the buck.
The matters have been referred to another department.	We passed the buck.
We decided to defer a decision to another meeting.	We're looking for someone to pass the buck to.
Can I get back to you on that one?	I don't understand one word of what you're saying.
I'm afraid I'm awfully busy at the moment.	I have a busy golf schedule.
I wasn't aware that was going on.	I didn't think anyone would find out about that.
I'll have to give it some consideration.	No.
My hands are tied.	No.
With the continual financial cutbacks and the general economic recession, I am afraid that I can't see much chance of any such proposal actually getting through the system.	No.

You've got everything you could want in life: a house, kids, a video cassette recorder. So, of course, you want to show it all off to other people. You decide to do this in the standard Australian way—by having a dinner party.

T·R·A·N·S·L·A·T·I·N·G
DINNER PARTY
BULLSH*T

```
RAGE AT SUE'S PLACE
BYO.
SAT 18TH. 8 p.m.
```

Now, we all know that no self-respecting Australian would dare arrive at this party before 9 p.m. And they will be considered too early.

The only way to get Australians to arrive on time to a party is to offer them a bribe: free drinks or dinner.

The purpose of Australian non-dinner parties is for people to meet while music is being played so loudly that no one can notice all the Bullshit that is being spouted. On the other hand, the purpose of Australian dinner parties is not to eat but to talk.

The main dish served at any Australian dinner party is Bullshit, lashings and lashings of Bullshit. One advantage of this is that it makes the rest of the meal taste a lot better.

GREETING EACH OTHER

TRANSLATION

GREETING EACH OTHER	TRANSLATION
How are you?	For God's sake, please don't really tell me how you are, that would be so boring.
Fine.	I'm terrible but why should you have to suffer too?
I'm great!	I'm not really great but I want you to feel lousy about the fact that I'm apparently doing so well.
We met at the last dinner party here, didn't we?	I've forgotten your name.
Your wife's looking well.	I'd like to jump your wife.
It's from all the running around she does.	She's too busy to fool around, so there.

Your husband's looking well.

I'd like to jump your husband.

Yeah, I think it's because he's slowed down since he had his heart scare.

He's too fragile to fool around, so there.

ABOUT YOUR OWN LOOKS

TRANSLATION

I've been on a diet.

I know I'm overweight but please don't say anything about it.

Oh, this old thing.

Yes, it is a wonderful dress, isn't it.

just a little thing I picked up recently

a phenomenally expensive outfit

It was casual, wasn't it?

I thought Stubbies and thongs would be all right.

ABOUT THE OTHER PERSON'S LOOKS

TRANSLATION

That's a really colourful outfit.

Yuk, how horribly tasteless.

You've lost some weight, haven't you?

You haven't put on any weight.

You look really well.

You have a tan.

You look really relaxed.

You're underdressed for the occasion.

Don't you look spiffy.

You're overdressed for the occasion.

You seem a little tired.

God, you're looking old.

WHAT THE COOK SAYS ABOUT THE MEAL

TRANSLATION

somewhat experimental	a failure
nouvelle cuisine	not enough
I hope you've got an appetite.	I made too much.
I hope you're hungry.	You'll need to be hungry to eat this.
a little spicy	The top of the chilli powder fell off.
I made it again because you said you liked it so much last time.	This is the only dish I know how to make.

WHAT THE GUESTS SAY ABOUT THE MEAL

TRANSLATION

good	bland
interesting	awful
very interesting	really, really awful
Only you could have created something like that.	unbelievably awful
unusual	awful in a new and different way
imaginative	awful in a very original way
fascinating	awful in an indescribable way
I enjoyed it.	I have no taste.

More spicy than I'm used to, but I really enjoyed it.

It removed the roof of my mouth.

I couldn't eat another bite.

I couldn't swallow another mouthful.

I'm stuffed.

I'm ill.

What's for dessert?

Can I have some ice-cream to take the taste away?

ABOUT THE KIDS

TRANSLATION

Young Johnny is doing very well at school.

Johnny goes to school almost every day.

My Margaret is going through one of those stages.

Margaret has had a nervous breakdown.

Robert's excellent at sports.

Robert is a dimwit.

Cynthia is taking her time settling down at a new school.

She failed her exams.

Arthur's the talented one of the bunch.

Arthur is the least moronic.

Mark has just gone girl-mad.

Mark wants us to buy him a panel van.

Glenda's just discovered boys.

I think she's sleeping around.

You can't tell them anything though, can you.

They're doing the same stupid things that I did at their age.

They don't listen.

I don't listen to them and they copy that.

They have to learn for themselves.

God my life's boring at the moment. I wish I was that age again.

ABOUT THE JOB

TRANSLATION

It's not too bad at the moment.

It's boring but safe.

Frankly, I'm a bit bored with it after all these years.

They keep passing me over for promotion.

I have changed my job actually.

I got sacked.

I've got a great new job.

They haven't spotted how shiftless I am yet.

I'm in line for a bit of a promotion.

again

ABOUT THE HOLIDAY

TRANSLATION

We're going to go somewhere different this year.

We're going away for the first in years.

We've got a little place up the coast.

We own a caravan.

Don't you find it's such a hassle organising the kids, the house, the dog?

We can't afford to go away.

ABOUT POLITICS

TRANSLATION

Let's face it, all politicians are wankers

I vote Labor.

DINNER PARTY BULLSH*T

We've got to be more conscious of our political rights and responsibilities.

I'm a wanker.

I don't think the dinner table is the right place to discuss politics.

We vote Liberal.

We don't know how lucky we are in this country.

We may be miserable here but at least we've got the right to whinge about how miserable we are.

With all due respect . . .

I am about to insult you.

ABOUT POSSESSIONS

TRANSLATION

Personally, I hate having a telephone in my car.

But I love boasting about it.

The new swimming pool is a lot of trouble.

But at least it gets the kids out of the house.

We're thinking of putting on some home extensions for the kids.

But personally I'd prefer giving them the house and running away.

We're thinking of doing some redecorating.

The house is falling apart.

ABOUT LEISURE-TIME ACTIVITIES

TRANSLATION

We're too busy to have time for a hobby.

We've given up sex.

My husband's really into his home computer.

My husband is a nerd.

74

My husband's so clever with his hands.

Except in bed.

I've taken up jogging.

I got sick of my wife's jibes about my beer belly.

I've taken up squash.

My wife has stopped giving me sex and pounding the ball helps me relieve my frustration.

FAREWELLS

TRANSLATION

I guess we'd better get a move on.

We've stayed the socially correct amount of time, haven't we?

Some of us have to work tomorrow.

which will be a nice change for me

Drive carefully.

You're pissed.

Thanks for a lovely meal.

Thank you for a meal I survived.

It was nothing really.

It was worse than nothing, really.

We'll have to have you over sometime soon.

Revenge! Revenge!

Finally, your mind and body can't take it any more. All those years of coping with Bullshit have taken their toll. You or one of your family gets ill, perhaps you even need an operation, and now you encounter the politest and the most revered Australian Bullshitter of them all—the Aussie Doctor.

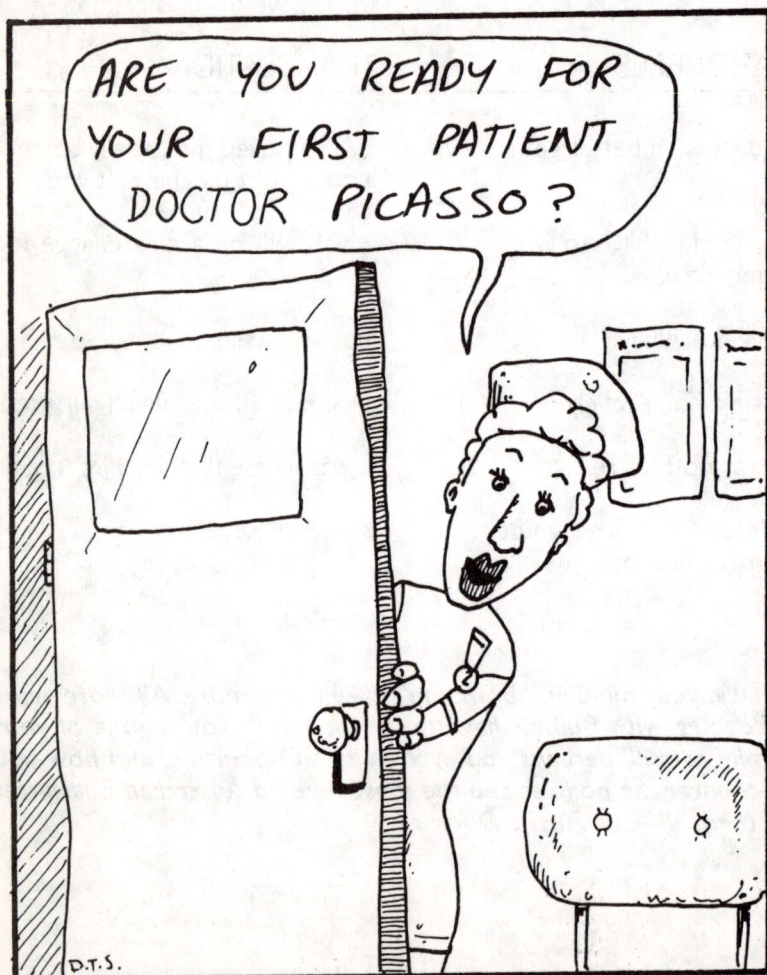

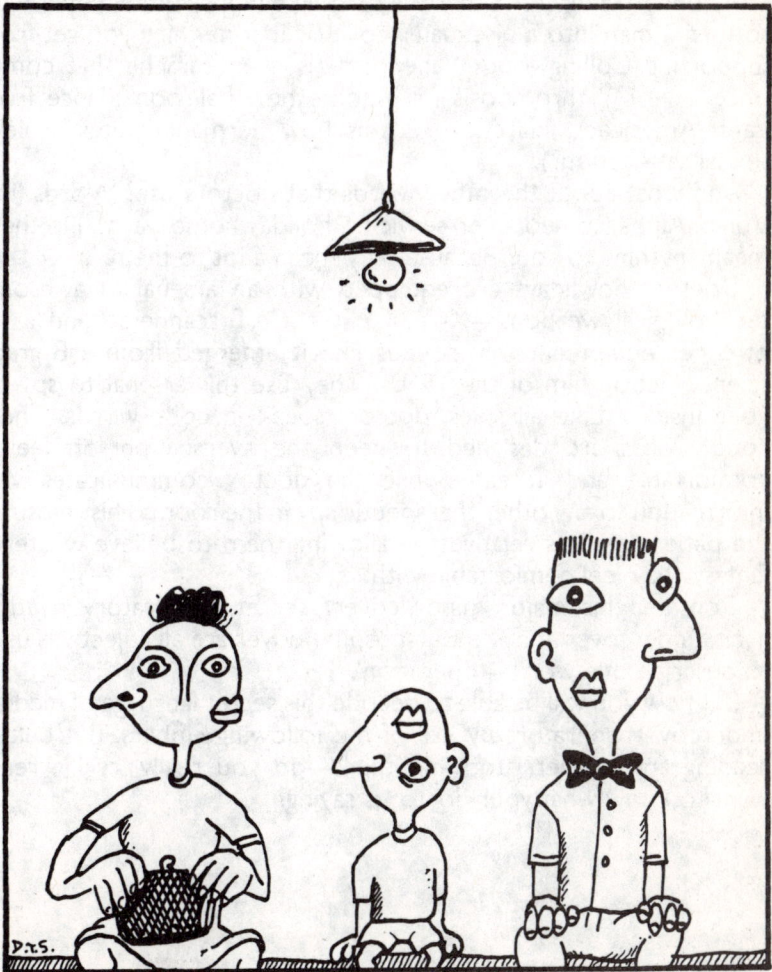

We have all heard of the Hippocratic oath—it is something that doctors take. And, as they don't prescribe it for their patients, it is probably very good for you.

But you don't know what 'hippocratic' means do you? Does it mean 'good for large, slow mammals with big round nostrils and piggy little ears that like to hang out around waterholes in South Africa'? You don't know, do you?

In fact there are a lot of words that your doctor uses that you don't understand, aren't there? Words like biopsy (is it an operation to turn a man into a bisexual?), colic (is it something you get from supporting Collingwood?), aneurism (is it an earache that comes once a year?), thrombosis (is it some new ballroom dance from Latin America?), infarction (is this how hermaphrodites achieve sexual satisfaction?).

And what about the other words that doctors use? Words like: Volvo, Alpha Romeo, over-servicing, holiday home, yacht. Do these mean anything to you? Because they mean a lot to them.

Doctors nowadays are equipped with an arsenal of awesome technological weapons—X-rays, EEGs, CAT scanners—and a lot of other equipment that sounds like it emerged from a B-grade science fiction film of the 1950s. They use this arsenal to spy on your insides. Like all spies, doctors speak in code words. These code words are designed to keep the average person feeling comfortable and at ease while the doctor communicates vital information to any other therapeutic spy in the room. This reassures the patient and his relatives by allowing them to believe whatever fantasy they feel comfortable with.

Consider this: major, minor, covert, secret, exploratory, routine, illicit, undercover and without-hospital-cover are all adjectives used to describe one word—'operation'.

But now you will be able to decode this secret language of medical undercover operators by use of the following ciphers. But before reading any further, stop and think—do you really, really, really want to know what your doctor is saying?

WHAT THE DOCTOR SAYS BEFORE THE OPERATION

TRANSLATION

I think we should get a second opinion.	You've got something so serious I don't want to take responsibility.
We might run a few tests.	I'm stumped; I don't know what the hell you've got.
an unusual complaint	a profitable complaint
minor surgery	The anaesthetist and I will be discussing our sex lives throughout the entire operation.
major surgery	I have checked that my malpractice insurance is up to date.
a routine procedure	a dangerous, tricky operation
exploratory surgery	We may have to rip a few things out.
just put you under and fix you up	major thoracic surgery
a radical operation	We are going to chop out large parts of you.
We may have to perform some corrective surgery.	You look like the elephant man.
You realise this procedure is purely elective.	God, you're a vain bastard.
There is absolutely nothing for you to worry about.	There is plenty for us to worry about.

We'll just fix up your waterworks.	You will need a catheter for the next six months.
There are modern alternative ways.	You will need a colostomy bag for the rest of your life.
I think I should leave you some time to discuss this with your wife.	After this operation, you will be impotent for the rest of your life.
I'll get a nutrition consultant to see you.	You're fat.
I'm only relieving here.	I don't know what the hell I'm doing.
I won't be a moment.	I won't be a moment; I will be much, much longer.
There will be some slight scarring.	You will look like Sylvester Stallone at the end of Rocky I.
This won't hurt at all.	This won't hurt *me* at all; you, however, will be in agony.
This won't hurt you a bit.	This won't hurt you a bit; it will hurt you a lot.
We'll keep an eye on that.	We'll wait until it gets really bad.
We're just waiting on the results of the test.	Stop pestering me; I don't know what's wrong.
The last time this operation was performed . . .	This operation has only ever been done once before.
I'd like to have a word to your spouse.	The test results have come back.
This might feel a little cold.	If you were an Eskimo this would feel a little cold.

You might feel a slight prick.

You might feel a slight prick; probably you will feel a searing stab.

Worrying about it won't do you any good.

Worrying about it won't do you any good; in fact, nothing at all could do you any good.

Please sign these forms.

Please sign away the right to sue me if I botch the operation.

WHAT THE DOCTOR SAYS AFTER THE OPERATION

TRANSLATION

We decided you didn't need these.

Here are the extra things we ripped out of you while you were under.

While we were there we just thought we'd fix up a few things.

You're falling apart inside.

You're doing just fine.

You're still alive.

We're all very pleased with your progress.

You're still alive—much to our surprise.

a satisfactory condition

unlikely to die today

a stable condition

the heart is still beating

a critical condition

could drop off any second

improving condition

less likely to die today than he was yesterday

The operation was more complicated than expected.

We failed.

nothing more we can do
for you

You are going to die.

These things come and go.

You have twelve months left to
live.

We can't make predictions.

You have six months left to live.

We don't know how long
you have left.

three months tops

That's about all we can do
for you. You may as well go
home to your family.

a fortnight, if you're lucky

We'll just top you up with
a little blood.

Make your will within the next
two hours.

Now it's a case of trial
and error.

Expect a slow, lingering death.

We can't really give you any
time scale.

You could last twenty years but
my money is on you dropping
dead on the way out of the office.

We'll just have to wait
and see.

Surprise us all—get better.

It takes a little time for
your body to remedy itself.

Have you tried prayer?

You must be patient.

Learn to enjoy pain.

You can't always see the
results straightaway.

Sometimes you never see any
results.

If you have any repeat of the
symptoms please come
back and see me.

We haven't really fixed you up
but we have our fingers crossed.

We'll see how you go on this programme.	You'll hate this regimen but you're just going to have to suffer.
You have a growth.	You're dying of cancer.
We've decided on a different tack in your treatment.	I botched your diagnosis the first time.
This is a new drug from overseas with less side effects.	This is an experimental drug.
These tablets can't be taken orally	Take these and shove them up your arse.
It will be a little sore.	It will be a little sore in some places; the rest of your body will be in agony.
We've got some new drugs. If you feel anything unusual, let me know.	They have bizarre side effects; you may grow hair in odd places.
It's important for the final year students to have some hands-on experience.	We want these first-years to have a grope of your body.
I'll be handing you over to the physio.	I'm washing my hands of you.
It's amazing how you learn to adjust to these sorts of things.	Learn to love your colostomy bag.

WHAT THE DOCTOR SAYS TO THE RELATIVES

TRANSLATION

He was late entering theatre.	He was on the table three hours longer than expected because he's falling apart inside.

The patient slept well.	We bombed him out on sleeping tablets.
He's eating and drinking well.	At least his mouth works.
He's up and about.	He hasn't had a relapse yet.
With your son's bump, you may notice a few unusual behaviour patterns.	He will dribble saliva for the rest of his life.
He is emotionally disturbed.	He's ga-ga.
We've put your son on some new hormones.	We have chemically castrated him to protect small children.
Your daughter may need a psychological consultation.	She thinks she's Caligula.
He's a bit confused.	He just bashed up three nurses.
Have you noticed any unusual behaviour in your son?	He's a drug addict.
Would you and your family step into this room for a minute?	We've had to cut something off him.
What religion are you?	He's dead.

Eventually you find a way to escape your doctor and all his euphemistic Bullshit. You die. And so finally you leave all that Bullshit behind forever. Or do you?

T·R·A·N·S·L·A·T·I·N·G
FUNERAL
BULLSH*T

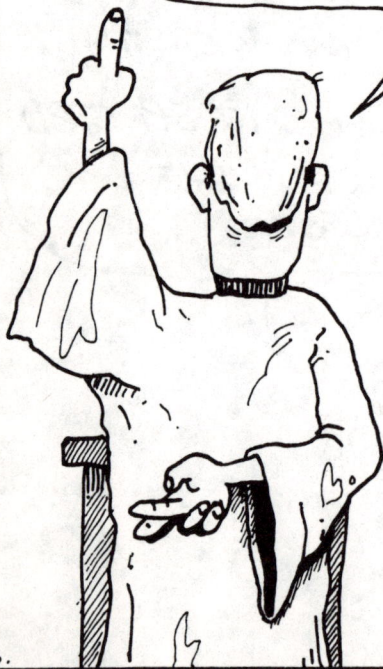

WHAT THEY SAY ABOUT THE DECEASED	TRANSLATION
a respected citizen	a person
beloved mother	she had children
will be sorely missed	owes money
left behind this world of cares and problems	is dead
she was a pillar of the community	made jam for stalls
generous to all	gave at doorknock appeals
lived life to the fullest	slept around
always put the family first	owned their own home
a person of enormous compassion	owned a dog
worked hard all his life	had a job
had to face many trials and always did so with dignity and quiet strength	His kids were on hard drugs.
left her family well provided for	had life insurance
died with dignity	did not have cancer
a good mate to his friends	drank heavily
a jovial, good-humoured woman	fat

lived his life with charity towards all and malice toward none	a wimp
a credit to his parents	passed HSC
loved life	drank, smoked and told dirty jokes
taken suddenly from his loved ones	had a heart attack
battled bravely through a long, painful illness and has now found peace	died